Crabapples

Homes around the world

Bobbie Kalman

Crabtree Publishing Company

Crabapples

created by Bobbie Kalman

for Lynda and Chris

Editor-in-Chief
Bobbie Kalman

Writing team
Bobbie Kalman
Petrina Gentile
David Schimpky

Managing editor
Lynda Hale

Editors
Tammy Everts
Janine Schaub

Computer design
Lynda Hale
David Schimpky

Color separations and film
Dot 'n Line Image Inc.

Printer
Worzalla Publishing Company

Illustrations
Brenda Clark: page 4
Antoinette "Cookie" DeBiasi: pages 28, 30
Deborah Drew-Brook-Cormack: page 8

Special thanks to
Ken Tinker and Heather Halfyard; Ian Bethell and Nicholas Stanko; Samantha Crabtree; Versna, Kosal, and Victoria Chuop; and Danielle Gentile

Photographs
Jeanette L. Andrews-Bertheau:
    pages 4 (both), 12, 15 (bottom),
    22 (bottom)
André Baude: page 21 (top)
William Belsey: pages 16,
    17 (both)
Jim Bryant: pages 10 (both),
    11 (both), 13 (top), 18, 19,
    20, 22 (top), 23 (top)
Marc Crabtree: front cover, title
    page, pages 5 (top), 6 (bottom),
    21 (bottom), 23 (bottom),
    27 (bottom), 29 (top right)
Peter Crabtree: pages 29 (top left),
    30 (top)
GeoStock: page 30 (bottom)
Lori Hale: page 14
Heather Halfyard: page 9 (top left)
Bobbie Kalman: back cover, pages
    7 (both), 8, 24 (both), 25 (both)
    27 (top), 28 (bottom)
Maria Magnotta: page 28 (right)
Diane Payton Majumdar:
    page 9 (top right)
Berit Qundos: page 29 (bottom)
Mike Silver: pages 5 (bottom),
    13 (bottom)
Jan Sommerville: page 6 (top)
Donald Standfield: page 26
Ken Tinker: page 9 (bottom)
World Vision: page 28 (top left)

Crabtree Publishing Company

350 Fifth Avenue	360 York Road, RR 4	73 Lime Walk
Suite 3308	Niagara-on-the-Lake	Headington
New York	Ontario, Canada	Oxford OX3 7AD
N.Y. 10118	L0S 1J0	United Kingdom

Cataloging in Publication Data
Kalman, Bobbie, 1947-
    Homes around the world

(Crabapples)
Includes index.

ISBN 0-86505-609-9 (library bound)   ISBN 0-86505-709-5 (pbk.)
This book looks at various kinds of dwellings, including arctic homes, homes on stilts, homes on boats, and desert homes.

1. Dwellings - Juvenile literature. I. Title. II. Series: Kalman, Bobbie, 1947-   . Crabapples.

GT172.K35 1994   j392'.36   LC 94-22902
                                                      CIP

What is in this book?

What is a home?

Some houses are big. Some houses are small. Some teeter high up on stilts. Houses can be built of wood, mud or snow. They can even be tents that are on the go!

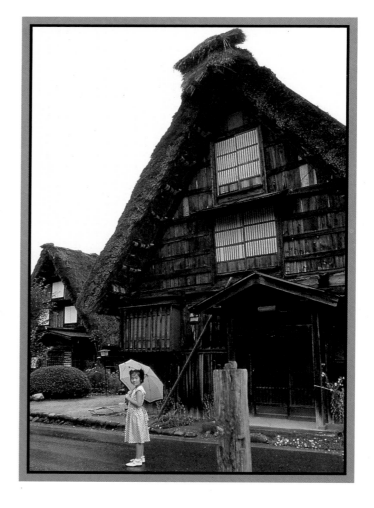

At home we feel safe and secure. Inside our homes we are sheltered from wind, rain, snow, and sun. Our belongings are also protected.

Homes are different all over the world. No matter where you live, there is no place like home!

Living in the city

Cities are full of people. Some live in houses, but there is not enough land for everyone to build a house.

Hundreds of people can live in an apartment building. Each one has floors and floors of homes. There are thousands of apartment buildings in cities!

Suburbs are communities that have grown outside cities. People who work in big cities often choose to live in the suburbs. The homes are larger and not as crowded together as city homes are.

Suburban homes often have front and back yards where children have room to play. Some have swimming pools.

In the country

Many people live in small towns and villages. Towns and villages are not as busy as cities because there are fewer people. The villagers or townspeople often know one another well.

Some people live in the country. Country homes are built in big open areas away from cities, towns, and villages. The closest neighbors are often miles away.

Some country homes are farmhouses. Farmers use the land around their home to grow crops or raise animals.

Simple homes

Some people live in **huts**. Huts are built in different ways. They can be made of mud, clay, or stones. Grass, branches, bark, and reeds are other materials used in building huts. Few huts have electricity or running water. Sometimes up to fifteen people live in one hut!

In some villages, each family shares a group of huts called a **compound**. Parents and children live in different huts. Would you like to live in a hut of your own?

Mountain homes

Mountain areas are rocky, windy, and cold. There are few trees. The people who live there must build sturdy homes.

Some people build homes right into the side of a mountain. The mountain shelters their home from strong winds.

Many **monasteries** have been built in the mountains. The people who live in monasteries spend their lives praying and studying religion. Being high up in the mountains makes some people feel closer to God.

Tropical homes

Tropical areas are hot all year. Green trees and beautiful flowers surround tropical homes.

During the rainy season in the tropics, some areas are flooded. In these wet areas, people build their homes on **stilts**. Stilts raise houses above water.

Arctic homes

In the past, the Inuit who live in the Arctic used **igloos** as their winter home. Igloos are made from bricks of snow. Today, igloos are used only as a temporary shelter during hunting trips. People do not live in them anymore.

Arctic residents now live in houses. Their homes are raised above the ground because the soil is frozen all year long. If the homes were built right on the ground, the heat from the floor would thaw the frozen soil, and the houses would sink.

In the winter, some people build a snow tunnel outside their home to keep out the icy wind.

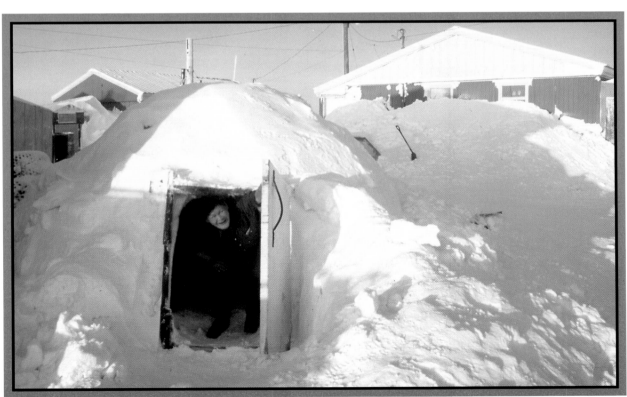

Desert homes

People who live in the hot, dry desert build homes that have thick walls. Thick walls keep rooms cool during the day. At night, when it can get very cold, the thick walls keep the heat inside the home.

Desert homes are made of sandstone, mud, or **adobe** bricks. Adobe is sun-dried soil or clay. Sticks are added to the walls to make them stronger.

Homes on the go!

Can you imagine camping outside every night? **Nomads** do! Nomads are people who move from one place to another. The people in this photograph live in tents. When the rainy season begins, they camp out in the desert. During the summer months, they live in areas where their animals can find fresh grass to eat.

Some African people build huts that come apart easily. When it is time to move, they carry their homes with them.

If you like to stay at home and travel at the same time, a trailer home is for you! A trailer home can be attached to a car or truck and driven to a new location any time!

Homes on water

People live in floating homes for many reasons. Some cannot find homes on land because the cities are too crowded. Others make a living on the water. They catch fish or take tourists on boat tours.

Floating homes can look just like the homes built on land. Many have electricity and running water. Some owners park boats beside their homes.

Nicola's home

Nicola is nine. She has lived on a sailboat since she was six months old. She has sailed to many places and met people around the world. She finds friends wherever she goes.

Nicola has several chores. She helps with the cleaning. She washes the dishes and hangs out the wash. She raises the flag and can operate the boat's radio.

Nicola's parents are her teachers. She has two hours of school each day. She does some of her lessons on the computer.

Nicola loves her floating home. She wakes up to a new adventure each day!

Second homes

Some people have a second home where they spend their vacations or relax on the weekends. A second home might be a cabin in the woods, a cottage in the country, or a house on the beach.

People who travel use hotels, apartments, or boats as a temporary home.

Some children live at camp during the summer. Others spend ten months of the year at a school that is far from home. They live in the school **residence** where they share a room with other students.

It is fun to live in a home away from home, but there is no place like your real home!

Children at home

Take a peek into the lives of children around the world. Find the location of their homes on a globe or in an atlas.

Suryatining lives outside a city in Indonesia. Her home does not have running water. She washes dishes outdoors using water from a well.

Luisa lives in a village in Italy. She takes care of her grandmother's chickens, roosters, and rabbits.

Scott, in the dark blue t-shirt, lives in Toronto, Canada. His many cousins are helping him celebrate his birthday. Some of them are visiting from the United States.

Storm lives in Ghana, Africa. Pretty flowers grow around her city home. Her dress is as colorful as the flowers!

Nicholas's home is on an island in the Bahamas. Nicholas loves to play tennis and swim in the pool.

Jonas and Victor's home is in Sweden. They live in a suburb of Stockholm.

Mansion or shack?

Some people live in comfortable homes and even mansions, but many live in poorly built shacks. There are homeless people in cities around the world. The government tries to help by building simple homes for them.

People who live in shacks are not always unhappy. Any house, whether a mansion or a shack, can be a happy home!

Words to know

adobe Sun-dried soil or clay
atlas A book of maps
clay Wet earth that hardens when it dries or is baked
compound A group of huts
desert A hot, dry place
globe A sphere on which a map of the world is drawn
igloo A dome-shaped home made of snow
Inuit The native people of the Arctic region
mansion A large, luxurious house

monastery A building where people in a religious community live together
nomad A person who moves his or her home from place to place
reed A tall, thick grass that grows in wet places
sandstone Rock made up of grains of sand
stilts Posts used to raise a building above the ground
suburb A community outside a city
tourist A person who travels for fun

Index

What is in the picture?

1 2 3 4 5 6 7 8 9 0   Printed in USA   3 2 1 0 9 8 7 6 5 4